# JACK PAYS A VISIT

## MICHAEL MINASSIAN

ASSURE PRESS

ASSURE PRESS

An imprint of Assure Press Publishing & Consulting, LLC

www.assurepress.org

Publisher's Note: Assure Press books may be purchased for educational, business, or sales promotional use. For information please visit the website.

Jack Pays a Visit/ Michael Minassian— 1st ed.

Cover artwork: Painting by Christine Karapetian

Author Photo by Sue Minassian

ISBN-13: 978-1-954573-14-7
eISBN-13: 978-1-954573-15-4

## ACKNOWLEDGMENTS

I would like to thank the following fellow friends and poets for their support and input: Christine Irving, Liana Minassian, Michael Newell, Alan Walowitz, and Robert Wexelblatt.

Most of these poems (sometimes in different form) have previously appeared in the following periodicals, to whose editors grateful acknowledgement is made:

*Aurorean*

*Comstock Review*

*Corvus*

*Good Works Review*

*Lotus-eater Magazine*

*Sheila-na-gig*

*Verse-Virtual*

# PREFACE

My uncle, Jack Karapetian (1925-1994), wrote under the pen name of Hakob Karapents. Born in Tabriz, Iran, Jack was a prolific Armenian-American writer who wrote almost exclusively in Armenian. Through the years, he encouraged my writing and often read my poems and short stories, making comments and suggestions. After he retired and moved to Connecticut, we would go for long walks and discuss the craft of writing. I still consider him my muse and mentor.

# CONTENTS

*Dedicated to my grandparents, survivors of the Armenian Genocide.*

# JACK PAYS A VISIT

# THE DOGS OF PERSIA

Pausing to light his pipe,
Jack looks at me over the flame
and curves his eyebrows upward,
as if he would ask a question
but instead tells me about the novel
he is writing about his university days
in Tehran and his first love
which ended badly, he says,
after he burnt down her father's house,
preferring the symbolic gesture to refusals,
blood oaths, and false anger.

"Besides," he says, "I didn't love her anymore."

We walk in silence for a while
stopping to listen to a bird cry
to its mate, a plaintive wail in the sudden
sun drenched clearing just before
we come upon the tangle of blueberry bushes ripe with fruit;
the dense fragrance of berries reaching us first.

Then Jack tells me how he paid the penalty
with his own exile and journey to America
leaving behind his father, friends, and favorite dogs.
"There's always a price to pay," he says.
And we haggle over who will taste the first blueberries,
then the way truth is revealed to the wounded,
next the stewardship of words and their meaning,
like poets we want to know why there's no passion
left in life or love, in song or speech;
trading truths & small lies, then abandoning language,
until finally I realize we are bargaining for life itself,
exchanging the stars for the lights

of a far-away city, and the sound of raindrops
for the wounded barking of long forgotten dogs.

## WAKING UP IN AMERICA

Secluded in Eastern Connecticut, my uncle
hikes the woods around his house, past the barn
into the long field that leads to a pond
where we skim rocks and watch hordes of insects,
red and gold leaves floating in lazy circles,
and a migration of clouds reflected in the surface.

He tells me to write my life,
"write about your regrets," he urges,
but I realize he is talking about himself.

Later that night in the next room,
I hear Jack talking in his sleep
and lean my head against the wall
then fall asleep standing up,
walking backwards out of his dreams,
writing short poems with long sentences.

In the morning, I translate his stories
from Armenian to English, sensing
remorse in the lives he re-imagines:
his childhood in Iran, the early years
as an immigrant/student in Kansas and the Bronx,
marriage, the birth of my cousins,
and his self-exile amid cold New England winter nights;
his stories crowded with chance meetings
with beautiful women, dead Persian poets,
and philosophers who blossom like flowers
then fade away like a door closing
behind a blue veil the color of the swimming pool
in the back yard, six thousand miles from Tehran.

# CONVERSATION IN CONNECTICUT

On this crisp fall afternoon,
Jack swings the axe
in one smooth motion,
splitting the logs one after another;
gazing out past the driveway
to the stand of bent white elms;
he pauses, then hands me the axe
as if he were asking me to write
a chapter in his latest novel.

"When I left Tehran," he says,
"the only thing my father said
was that we would talk again."

As I swing the axe down,
the loud *thwack* startles the crows
hiding among the elms,
and I imagine I can hear them talking
in a low murmur like smoke curling
under a door or a crowd at an airport
saying a final farewell to a young relative.

Jack grunts and seems to dismiss
the crows with a wave of his hand,
then fills his pipe, and lights it,
closing his eyes, and I wait for the end
of the story that I know will come,
and he says, "Of course, we never did."

Later, we stack the wood into long piles
next to the back door, and I build a fire
in the stone fireplace in Jack's study
while he clacks his ancient Remington
creating his father's inner world:

"Something has to burn," he says,
"if there is going to be light."
and I picture the words flaring into flame
on the page like love annihilating loss
or black crows scattering against gun metal gray clouds
on their way to an ocean too vast to cross.

## A FAMILY OF GIANTS

Hiking through the woods,
at the end of the day,
Jack and I follow
the slow incline of the path
between the trees whose leaves,
already heavy with color,
scatter yellow and gold
in the slightest breeze.

At the top of the hill,
Jack points to the lake
in the distance below
and tells me an Armenian
folk tale about a family
of giants who lived in caves:
the females with breasts so large
they flung them over their shoulders
and the men with lips so full,
that one touched the earth
and the other reached the sky.

"What do we call the world?"
he asks, "When the giants
no longer reveal
themselves?"

As we walk, he tells me
that when he first
came to this country
he shaved his moustache
and trimmed his eyebrows
so he would look
less like a foreigner.

"That's why I became
a writer," he said.
"When I spoke,
there was no way
to cut off my accent."
Who wouldn't want
to be an American? he adds.

Then we turn and make
our way back through
the woods to the house
where my aunt waits;
following our long shadows
in the afternoon sun
as they crossed in front
of us on the road home.

## THE POND IN THE WOODS

Near the end of our trek
through the woods, Jack and I
come upon the small pond
across the street from his house.

A thin sheen
of green pond scum
covers the surface,
and a rusted metal sign
warns **No Swimming**
as if anyone would dive
into that mordant muck.

Jack insists the sign
is meant to be ironic
or at least a metaphor.
"If you swim in that pond,"
he adds, "you'll find it has
no beginning or end."

I tell him I can see the other
shore that ends in a stand
of white birch trees
bent over in the wind.

"Just another metaphor," he says
and I look at him,
his hair as white as the clouds
skittering across the sky above us
and wonder when did he grow old.

Later, we sit in his study
drinking cups of strong coffee
surrounded by Jack's manuscripts

and letters; he places his lips
on my forehead.
"I prefer the symbol
rather than the word," he says.

Just after dark, he takes
me back to the pond,
our way lit by a single flashlight
until we reach the same shore
and watch the fireflies
rise above the water
as infinite as the stars
with no beginning and no end.

# NAMING THE OLIVE TREE

Jack and I walk in the woods
scratching time like an old 45 record,
naming each section of the path
after our favorite poets:
Gibran, Rumi, Shakespeare, & Whitman
forming the boundary from the barn
to the blueberry patch.

Along the way back home
we watch the rain descend
& wonder which of these trees
will fall in the next storm
or burst apart from a lightning strike:
burnt paper on which to write a song.

Lighting his pipe, Jack told me the story,
of when he was a young boy in Tehran
& how he heard a dervish walking past the garden wall,
singing *ghazals* and crying out to his lost love;
in the morning they found him hanging
from the branches of an olive tree:

*"When I first saw you, standing under the olive tree*
*How did the earth not stop spinning, under the olive tree*

*My lips yearning like a single drop of water in a desert*
*for your rose to bloom, the moon to blush, under the olive tree*

*I whisper your name on the walls of the wind*
*My tears to salt the earth, the mud, under the olive tree*

*like rain falling backwards from death to birth,*
*my sobs a song only I could hear, under the olive tree."*

## SOME BOOKS

Jack calls me on the telephone
to say he has mailed me a copy
of his latest novel –
"Be sure to tell me
what you think," he says.

And I remember the time we came out
of a movie theater
and overheard a couple arguing
in the parking lot – catching
every third or fourth word
slicing through the harsh winter air:
"you used to…"
"she doesn't like it when you…"
"so humiliating…."

Then the sound of a slap reaches us,
and the woman drives off leaving
her husband/boyfriend/lover
shivering red-faced under the streetlight.
Jack offers him a ride and I expect
the guy to say no, but he accepts.

Later, after we drop him off,
Jack sees two of his novels are missing
from the back seat, a few shreds of paper
on the floor of the car.
"It's OK," he says,
"some books are eaten to remember,
        some are eaten to forget."

# FAMOUS UNKNOWN PERSONS

Jack drums his fingers on the steering wheel
while I watch the exit ramps speed by
like a tape reel on fast forward,
looking for some kind of sign
or message written in the code
of interstate numbers or hidden
symbol in the names of highways or roads:

Jack is the first to break the silence,
"You and I," he says, "are famous
unknown persons." He pauses,
then continues, "Without us,
the whole earth,
the universe might disappear."

Then I repeat my name, then Jack's,
next I recite all the names
in our family, Armenian, American,
Persian, and the names of all
the homesick along the highways
and back roads of America.

We drive along, the radio
tuned to a talk show,
the constant murmur of voices
merging with traffic noise, whistling wind,
the sound of the disappearing landscape,
and famous unknown persons,
history's hitchhikers, trailing behind.

# NAMING THE WORLD

Hiking the woods
Jack and I come to
a field of wildflowers
and a flock of birds
murmuring overhead.

Sharpening a blade of grass
he asks if I could name
the parts of the world
what would I call the air,
clouds, birds, and grass.

Instead, I asked him
what name he would give
himself, what name
did he have before birth?

Isn't that the same thing?
he said, then called
the earth, clouds, and sky
by their Armenian names.

Perhaps the ankles of the trees
visible in the lifting fog
confused the birds
who, stricken with amnesia,
broke formation
and scattered in the wind.

## TO LIVE FOREVER

Jack and I are sweeping out the old barn
my cousin used as an art studio:
brushes stiff with dried paint
and clotted palettes sit on an old table
next to an easel leaning to the left
like an old man being pushed by the wind.

Behind some half-finished canvases
stacked up in a corner of the barn
I find dozens of dead bees—
*They look like black and yellow thumbtacks*
I say, pushing them with a straw broom
and I wonder how long they've been there.

I tell Jack to be careful,
you can still be stung by a dead bee,
but he waves me off:

In ancient Persia, he says,
bees were cultivated without stingers,
Kings used honey to reward
servants and the nobility.

Learning to listen
to the tongues of the bees
Kings believed death
was only a rumor,
expecting to live forever.

Outside, dark clouds piled up
like a wreck on the turnpike
and thunder rattled
the windows of the barn—
I sweep up the bees
and ask them to speak one last time.

# JACK PAYS A VISIT

Sitting in a coffee shop I notice
out of the corner of my eye
my uncle's reflection in the window.

He raises his thick gray eyebrows
and mouths the word *so-*
that's when I remember
he's been dead for 20 years.

I close my eyes
hoping he will go away,
but when I look again
he is sitting across the table
and tells me he's haunted
by the ghosts of Persian poets
and forgotten deities.

In ancient times, even after death,
poets and heralds wandered
from town to town
reciting the deeds of heroes
and the cruelties of the gods.

*Don't write about the dead*, I hear
him say just before he disappears,
his advice too late:
he has been haunting
my poems for years.

My uncle always said he preferred
symbols instead of words
the tiger's orange gaze
the tongues of stars
the hunger of the rain.

## CORRESPONDENCE

Alice and I send letters back and forth
no longer depending on email or cell phones,
preferring instead handwritten notes
we set out in cursive, recalling
penmanship lessons,
& the scratch of pen on paper
as if we could rearrange time,
bringing back my grandparents,
our favorite cousins,
her husband Jack,
dismantling whatever remains:

Distrusting even words
we turn instead to symbols & stick
figures until we understand
each other's language of forgotten
moments, the vocabulary of a single
line drawn on a blank page.

## ABOUT THE AUTHOR

Michael Minassian was born in New York City and grew up in New York and New Jersey. In addition to living in Florida, California, Connecticut, North Carolina and Texas, he lived and taught overseas in England, Jamaica, Saudi Arabia, and South Korea.

For over 30 years he was a member of the English Department at Broward College in South Florida. He also studied and served as a guest tutor for ten years at Cambridge University's Summer Study Program in the UK.

His poems and short stories have appeared recently in such journals as *The Comstock Review*, *Live Encounters*, *Lothlorien Poetry Journal*, *Poet Lore*, and *Chiron Review*. He is also a Contributing Editor for Verse-Virtual. His chapbooks include poetry: *The Arboriculturist* and photography: *Around the Bend*.

His poetry collections *Time is Not a River* and *Morning Calm* were both published in 2020. Michael's poetry manuscript *A Matter of Timing* won the 2020 Poetry Society of Texas' Catherine Case Lubbe Manuscript Contest (publication: Summer 2021).

Eye on Literature: an educational blog about culture & literature: http://eyeonliterature.blogspot.com

For more information: https://michaelminassian.com

 facebook.com/Michael-Minassian-123909083633

 twitter.com/mikial

 instagram.com/mikial57

## ALSO BY MICHAEL MINASSIAN

*A Matter of Timing*, 2021 (poetry)

*Time is Not a River*, 2020 (poetry)

*Morning Calm*, 2020 (poetry)

Chapbooks:

*Chuncheon Journal*, 2019 (poetry)

*Around the Bend*, 2017 (photography)

*The Arboriculturist*, 2010 (poetry)